# The Zentrepreneur's Idea Log & Workbook

*"There is an idea for every time
and a time for every idea."*

Other Zentrepreneur Guides®
by Ron Rubin and Stuart Avery Gold

*Success at Life: How to Catch and Live Your Dream*

*Dragon Spirit: How to Self-Market Your Dream*

*Tiger Heart, Tiger Mind: How to Empower Your Dream*

*Wowisms: Words of Wisdom for Dreamers and Doers*

Also by Ron Rubin and Stuart Avery Gold

*Tea Chings: The Tea and Herb Companion*

NEWMARKET PRESS
New York

A Zentrepreneur's Guide®

# The Zentrepreneur's
# Idea Log & Workbook

**RON RUBIN** AND **STUART AVERY GOLD**

This book is published in the United States of America.

First Edition

1   2   3   4   5   6   7   8   9   10

ISBN 1-55704-641-7

QUANTITY PURCHASES

Companies, professional groups, clubs, and other organizations may qualify for special terms when ordering quantities of this title. For information, write Special Sales Department, Newmarket Press, 18 East 48th Street, New York, NY 10017; call (212) 832-3575; fax (212) 832-3629; or e-mail mailbox@newmarketpress.com.

www.newmarketpress.com

Design by Kevin McGuinness

Manufactured in the United States of America

At the authors' request, this book has been printed on acid-free paper.

# Acknowledgments

To the many consummate Zentrepreneurs who undertook the motions and the emotions needed for turning this book into a reality. A special thank you to Gina Amador, whose incredible talent and WOWerful design has provided the beautiful covers for all the Zentrepreneur Guides. Her spirit brings an ever-evolving life and character to the series. To Kevin McGuinness for the interior design tapestry which weaves around our words. To the marvelous Machiko for all of her brushed-stroked paintings which illumine and embody the entire idea of this book. To buzz bees John and Fauzia Burke, Katherine Beitner, and Marideth Post. To everyone at Newmarket Press for their fabulous and flawless efforts, especially Keith Hollaman for organizing it all into inked actuality. This is the sixth book we've worked on together—he is the best there is. To Harry Burton and Heidi Sachner for their clear attention and awesome focus on getting Zentrepreneur Guides to the world. And to the ever-present support of Paul Sugarman, Shannon Berning, Frank DeMaio, and to William Rusin and Dosier Hammond of W.W. Norton & Company.

To our matchless, one-of-a-kind publisher Esther Margolis, for her mind, her soul, and her strategic insight. She has been, and continues to be, our light at the end of the tunnel.

*For Zentrepreneurs creating a place for ideas.*
*It's what we do.*

# Keep Infinity in the
# Palm of Your Hand

*Do not doubt that a single idea can change the world,*
*it is the only thing that ever has.*

This book was born because of one certain undeniable fact...

An idea is a thing with feathers. They can fly away as easily as they come, gone, never to revisit you again. And because ideas are not in the habit of appearing by invitation only, nor do they have the knack for arriving impeccably on time, you have to be ready with a place for them to land when they come circling. Understand this, when God in all of Her wisdom decides to send you a thunderbolt of creative unfoldment, you better not let it get away. Better get it down. Quickly. Record it before it leaves you. You must. Even if you are in any and all ways golden, brilliant, and fabulously organized, not to mention miraculously blessed with an elephant's memory, I promise you that what enlivens and excites can be momentary and ephemeral if pen is not put to paper. Meaning, woefully:

Everyday, wonders slip though the cracks.

It's that simple. And that tragic. An idea is a nonrecurring phenomenon that can go like a streak and cannot be willed back into being. Albert Einstein, who was only sharper than all of us, said that the greatest idea that he ever had was the one that he forgot. In other very important words, sometimes greatness comes so quickly. The point to be polished here is that by writing down your ideas, and this is crucial, you catch them in their fragile beginning, creating their existence in tangible form, giving you the wondrous opportunity to go beyond the known and the unknown to deliver destiny.

Be a thinker-upper/writer-downer. Make visible the providential burst that comes to you from out of whatever glorious blue and seize its excitement. Embrace and celebrate it, allowing the inexplicable energy of the idea's potential to fill you with the positive feelings that can propel potent possibility. Seeing your idea on paper will permit you to travel beyond what is into an exhilarating world of what can be. Paying attention to inspiration and observation, allowing the sudden illumination of your creative visions, the whisperings of instinct to be captured and inked, is an invaluable practice that can actually allow things to happen. Creative people know this. And business people believe it....

An idea is the ancestor to every success.

Look around you—everything you see, every great-as-ever convenience of daily living we use and ultimately take for granted, all the technology, ritual, books, art, music, and entertainment we enjoy, began as a dawning, an inspiration, a creative vision that existed as a result of someone's imagination and intuition. Their idea. From the very beginning, since the ancients thought of using fire to flicker the darkness to Edison's idea for seeing the world in a different light, the capacity for allowing us to grab hold of an idea has been lurking latent inside each and every one of us, waiting to be welcomed. It is your ability to capture its calling that is the beginning of everything. And makes life in all ways splendid.

Ideas have a wonderful symmetry. You embrace an idea because you need an idea and because it needs you. So it is that ideas pervade our universe, always existing, waiting for our conscious participation, dedicating themselves to discovery until suddenly, Shazam, there it is. As an example to be mentioned here, when Newton got a noggin-knock from the apple, please understand, he didn't invent the idea of gravity—he merely discovered its already existence. Then what he wanted more than anything on earth was to get his idea down, since writing it down gave it genuine intellectual weight. Newton created a manuscript full of thoughts and honed observations regarding his discovery, before widening the world for the ages to his important findings. Same with the Google guys, Larry Page and Sergey Brin. In the quicksilver of the Internet, search engines were already in swing when the two Stanford University students knew and believed there was a more ultimate way, so they opened themselves to taking a greater creative look, putting plenty of ideas onto paper, trapping them, shaping them, nurturing them, giving their concepts expression, some soaring with success, others doing a crash-and-burn. And please do not light candles for these two toilers, all we're truly trying to show here is how a few-dollars notebook can end up harboring a billions-of-dollars idea.

With this very much in mind, be prepared for the finite notes that strike a chord and reverberate inside you. Listen to it. Grab hold of it. Shake it and see what falls out. Then, and this is paramount, quickly write it down before, with shocking speed, it shifts, alters, and goes thud, bouncing, never to return. Francis Bacon advocated, "A man would do well to carry a pencil in his pocket and write down the thoughts of the moment. Those that come unsought are commonly the most valuable and should be secured, because they seldom return." Ron and I say, "Never let a ready piece of paper be out of reach, since what would one be without the other?"

You simply must capture the teeming spark of an idea on paper so it can give birth to another, which unleashes a stream of other ideas that can support, enhance, and empower actions that help marshal manifestation of the idea into a materialized reality. So when you luck into an idea, put ink on paper, lock it in so you can lock it down. Go back to it again later to review and consider if it still excites and fills you with positive feelings and purpose. Because, in time, some ideas stiff as they unwind, while some remain such wonders the next time and the next time after the next time.

And if this seems like some off-the-wall suggestion, know that museums, universities, and private collections the world over house the imaginative jottings of Archimedes, Michelangelo, da Vinci, Copernicus, Picasso, the Wright brothers, and Einstein, just to name hardly any. Truth to know is that there exists a lengthy written trail of chance encounters, cultivated revelations penned by the hand of their creative greats. Tangible reminders of ideas recorded to ensure that they didn't get lost in the tumult of daily events. No wonder that since 1978, the Smithsonian and Rutgers University have been hard at work archiving the more than five million pages of ideas, notes, and other papers that Thomas Edison left behind. Fortunately for our hyper-inattentive world, Edison knew that a sharp mind deserves a sharp pencil.

And a portfolio of possibility.

What you must realize is that the simple act of writing down an idea is more than putting pen to paper, it is a very assertive way of endowing yourself with ascendancy, helping you to become a more powerful creative thinker, providing you with the infusion of certain confidence and emotional energy necessary to importantly acquire the ability to approach your life with a mindful sense of discovery, creativity, and imagination. The ability to visit with an idea can take you to places you've never been, never knew existed, allowing you to discern the oh-so-startling difference between being interested by something and being interested in something. The difference making all the difference, permitting only just the right idea to embrace you. Collecting your creative visions, inspirations, apparitions, and enthusiasms will reconnect you with your inner talents and gifts you've been ignoring. Understand, an idea, even the possibility of a dazzler, can fan the flames of your dreams and desires. It will uplift and inspire, filling you with zest and zeal to achieve whatever you dare to dream possible.

Imagine the unimagined—ideas come from a new way of thinking and believing. And acting.

The point to be made here is that by putting your ideas on paper you are programming yourself to accept the possibility of probability. By creating a home for cogency, you become a believer in your power to let something remarkable go out into the world.

Quick ramble...Ron and I know, and know well, how paramount it is to pen down ideas. Truth to tell, we've been around this block more than a time or two, and after so many years of creating and marketing so many products, we are wise and experienced hands who very much assign a great importance to inking ideas on paper. So with Zentrepreneur Guides now translated into many languages around the world, the reviews, articles, and interviews (thank luck) always terrific, we decided to approach the wizards at our publisher with this idea for this idea log and workbook, believing that such a thing can be a vital instrument of manifestation. A potent tool to assist in building the foundation and framework for empowering dreams. So when the powers that be gave us thirty minutes to articulate the necessity for such a thing, I took it (along with a swig of Kaopectate—my stomach churning with hope). And when the thirty minutes they promised turned into sixty minutes because of their keenness and then went clocking to ninety, there wasn't a scowl or a yawn from anybody when the pitching was done, because bright people always understand. The good ones do.

And so here it is, a place for grasping greatness. Drum roll, please... *The Zentrepreneur's Idea Log & Workbook*. A welcoming world to be carried with you to greet and befriend your thoughts, inspirations, pre-ideas, and *the* ideas. A sanctuary of solitude just for you, to record your creative intuition, proddings, views, and solutions. A place of privacy to go wandering, defining your ideas, strengths, to unashamedly dare to discover its faults and weaknesses, a space to see what works, what doesn't, why it doesn't, how maybe it can.

Keeping an idea log is to keep infinity in the palm of your hand. Regard it as a dimensionless repository to embrace the finite and the infinite, where connectives click, a very important way of knotting together authentic action and reaction.

Giving your idea a palpable presence is the very first step in looking at what wants to be looked at, transforming it from a flash of formless mental energy into a charge of physical purposeful energy. This is good since everything that makes up a visible viability is born from a quantum invisible equivalent. And if this seems like some new-age mumbo jumbo, ugh, then this is as good place as any to pause and discuss the theory that is at the spine of quantum mechanics.

Whoa.

Now before you hurl this book right through the window, know that we're going to spare you the blackboard stuff and use just the next couple of sentences to explain that Max Planck and Albert Einstein voiced the theory that the smallest fractions of matter have no physical basis. That they are in fact patterns made from the same, non-physical material—patterns of information waiting for the participation of consciousness. That consciousness is the basic unit of an idea. And that an idea is pure potentiality that seeks realization.

Translation...

Simply put, you will find it amazing, fascinating, reassuring, and absolutely faith-building when you begin to document and keep track of not only how many good ideas you can get ahold of, but much more remarkable is how many good ideas can get a hold of you.

Magical moments.

This *Idea Log & Workbook* is for you to put stuff in. To attach. To thicken. To make many notes. To make many more notes. To tinker. To zoom in. To elaborate. Cogitate. Deliberate. Ruminate. Validate. Expand. Expound. Stretch. Prune. Ponder. Review. Rewrite. Re-see. Restate. Go over your idea. Get under it. Begin to believe you can move a mountain. Believe you can move others. Know you can move yourself. Yesterday's idea is today's reality. Today's idea can be tomorrow's reality. Alas, no simple amusement, regard the *Idea Log & Workbook* as a practice, designed to provide you with an accumulating means and guidance that can take you places you have never been, never knew existed, a passage to paradise where if you follow it you can create your dream future. A comparative dynamic of this can be seen mirrored in the element of water. Water can be one drop, or if gathered together, it can become a large sea, teeming with life.

Forever creating.

Realize that you too are at all times sublime, each moment along life's journey standing at the crossroads of creative joy. In this grand world of ours, greatness is a birthright of each and every one of us. We need only to be prepared to welcome it. Be ready to be ready. You may not want to hear this, but this cannot be stated too often or too strongly, so we're going to put it in very large type:

# IT'S ALL UP TO YOU!

It is you, repeat, you, who must undertake the brave behavior that will empower your ideas. You who must dare to take the dares. You who must be prepared to penetrate the process. You who must become a provocateur of potential. If it's not broken . . . BREAK IT! The force of a new idea can overtake an old one. Pursue innovation. Out with the old ways of doing things—in with the view. Use your creative vision. Concoct the unconcocted. Dent the universe! Be a deliverer of D-I-F-F-E-R-E-N-T. Be a fantasy fanatic. Dream big. Size matters. Dream wild. Boundlessness matters. Dream WOW. Wackiness matters most. Delight in the openness of possibilities. Then, consecrate your creative vision by dedicating to give it shape and form. This is how ideas happen. This is how glorious creation takes place. Dream...Think...Act! Everything else is mythology. Period.

While some will never believe it unless they see it, Zentrepreneurs see it because they believe it.

I wrote in an earlier book that at first there is no road, it's only when a person begins it that it exists for others. And so it is with an idea. No matter what continent you live on, our planet is populated with decent human beings, waiting for magic in their lives, but they lack the comprehension of what it takes to provide for the homelessness that surrounds their ideas. So sad. Crushing too, since they believe that attaching themselves to the right idea can bring about great happiness, when truth to tell, attaching themselves to the right idea can only bring about a great beginning. *The Zentrepreneur's Idea Log & Workbook* is that, a veritable wellspring for great beginnings.

Important. Very.

Because for every idea there is a great beginning and for every great beginning there is an idea. Emerson said that everything is made from hidden stuff. He is one hundred and ten percent right. Between the world of what is and the world that can be, a great idea waits ready for you, if you would only make yourself ready for it.

Here's hoping you do...

*—Stuart Avery Gold*

An idea is a thing with feathers. They can fly away as easily as they come, gone, never to revisit you again.

*easily as they come*
*easily as they come*
*easily as they come*
*easily as they come*
*easily as they come*
*easily as they come*
*easily as they come*
*easily as they come*

*gone, never to revisit you*
*gone, never to revisit you*
*gone, never to revisit you*
*gone, never to revisit you*
*gone, never to revisit you*
*gone, never to revisit you*

thing with feathers They can fly away as gone, never to revisit you again.

easily as they come,
gone, never to revisit you again.

The Zentrepreneur knows that time is hard to find and easy to lose. Organize and prioritize. More than time management, learn to practice time awareness. Assign yourself a certain time of day to accomplish tasks, goals, and activities. For example, write e-mails, make important phone calls, or run errands during a specific blocked out space instead of trying to fit these actions in. This creates efficiency in your schedule. Important. Because the Zentrepreneur is serious about work and is serious about play. Thoreau said, "It is not enough to be busy. The question to always ponder is, what are we busy about?" Take the time to make the time to laugh more, and worry less. When you change the way you spend your time, the way you spend your time changes.

"It is not enough to be busy.

The question to always ponder is,

what are we busy about?"

Take the time

to make the time

to laugh more,

and worry less.

When you change the way you spend your time,
the way you spend your time changes

**Inside. Outside.** The true process of an idea has no beginning and no end. Like following the path of a circle, all thoughts lead back to the starting point, the experience of the journey changing your view of the idea that once was. A circle is infinite. A great idea is infinitely engaging.

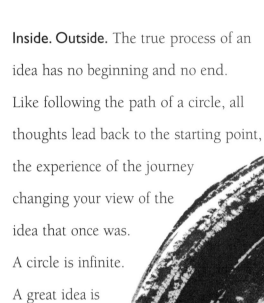

# Inside
Outside

# Listen for...

It is better to think a little than talk a lot. Listen for the great idea of your life. Hear and you will see. See and you will hear. Then wait for what the mind will do.

An idea is a calling that screams t

# The great idea of your life.

hose that quiet themselves long enough to listen.

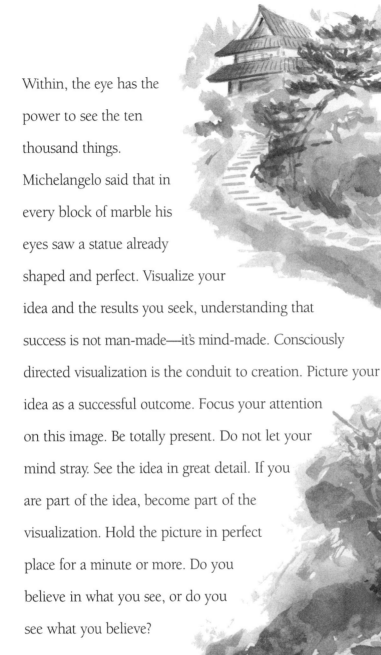

Within, the eye has the power to see the ten thousand things. Michelangelo said that in every block of marble his eyes saw a statue already shaped and perfect. Visualize your idea and the results you seek, understanding that success is not man-made—it's mind-made. Consciously directed visualization is the conduit to creation. Picture your idea as a successful outcome. Focus your attention on this image. Be totally present. Do not let your mind stray. See the idea in great detail. If you are part of the idea, become part of the visualization. Hold the picture in perfect place for a minute or more. Do you believe in what you see, or do you see what you believe?

# Do you believe in what you see, or

do you see what you believe?

When ore is heated by fire it changes to liquid. When the liquid is poured into the mold it takes the shape of a bell. When it is cooled and crafted, the bell is tested with a strike. It is then that the beauty of the bell resonates. The creation of an idea is no different.

IT IS YOU WHO MUST DARE TO TAKE THE DARES.

IT IS YOU WHO MUST BE PREPARED TO PENETRATE THE PROCESS.

To increase your intention, increase your attention. All that stands in the way of your great idea is the applied art of paying attention. An idea is not a problem to be solved, it is a mystery to be revealed. By paying attention Zentrepreneurs open their capacity to relate and create, inviting true discovery.

Target your talents. Attain new life skills. Always . . . Always . . . Always. Remember that talent comes naturally. Skill is an achievement of purposeful action, learned through study, training, and practice. What skills do you need to acquire? How will you acquire them? By when? Make a WorkList of where to go to develop skills. Course study, seminars, mentors, internships, volunteer work, books, audiotapes, DVDs, journals, magazines. Then take part in the process, energetically, happily, and methodically. To do is to be.

Gaze upon the invisible. Listen to the
silences between the sounds. This is
when ideas come to play.

Turn your vision of what can be
into the view that others see.

gaze

upon the

invisible.

isten

to the

lences

etween

he

ounds.

his is

hen ideas

ome to

ay.

Emanate radiance. Make way for truth and perception. Adding or subtracting sights and sounds in your immediate environment can enhance the contemplative power of your mind. Do away with clutter, add pleasing art, textures, colors, fragrant plants, scented candles, a tabletop water fountain, wind chimes. The Zentrepreneur is mindful of the senses and all that they can convey. Care and attention to the detail of your surroundings will provide an environment that cultivates care and attention to the detail of your ideas.

36

三十六

xxxvi

# MAKE A WORKLIST

of the things you can do to create an uplifting harmonious space for yourself.

Emanate radiance.

An idea is a seed
that needs to be
nourished by a
fertile mind.
What knowledge,
resources, support,
and skills will you
require to manifest
the idea?

# MAKE A WORKLIST

What knowledge, resources, support, and skills will you require to manifest the idea?

IT IS YOU WHO MUST BECOME A PROVOCATEUR OF POTENTIAL.

IF IT'S NOT BROKEN . . . BREAK IT!  DENT THE UNIVERSE.

The Zentrepreneur extols a brighter shade of gray and avoids living in a world of black and white. Seeing things in terms of black and white is to ignore the possibility of potential. Black blocks light. White invites shadow. The subtle vagaries of gray create both depth and space, allowing to view an idea with soul and spirit, truth, and freedom. Like the Zen suiboku paintings that adorn this book, the reality of the image you see goes beyond the brush of black on white and is found in the subtlety of gray. Thoroughly withdraw from distinctions. Shadows cling to form. Exploring the gray is to reflect perfectly and respond appropriately. An idea is the light inside the dark.

*Change, like the beauty of a flower, is*
# ordinary activity.

Good advice is always there for us,

if we are simply there for it.

While Western medicine insists that it is the brain that moves the body, the Zentrepreneur knows that it is the mind that moves the world. The ongoing trouble is that since always humans have tried to squeeze the mind into the brain, never realizing that it won't fit.

THE WAY OUT TO AN IDEA IS BY GOING IN.

Rise above the
ordinary.

Uncover wisdom.
Develop direction.
Become a
connoisseur of
capability. A catalyst
for change. Enable
yourself to take the
dares. Success is an
act of exploration.
A commitment to a
quest to be the best.

THE FORCE OF A NEW IDEA CAN OVERTAKE AN OLD ONE.

CONCOCT THE UNCONCOCTED.

While some make the mistake of wasting time and money on the process of positioning an idea, others understand that success comes from the process of positioning themselves.

Ideas are
opportunities.
Serendipitous
openings for glories
and joys, waiting
for that certain
individual whose
unique
time it
is to
deliver them out
of darkness.

A Zentrepreneur's
mind is limitless,
its potential
inexhaustible. And
once you understand
that the brain cannot
hold the mind, you
free yourself to turn
your dream into a
radiant reality.

# The mind is limitless;
## its potential inexhaustible.

Accept the ups
and downs as natural
events and use them
as welcome lessons
that facilitate
self-transcendence
and growth. Align
your idea with
nature's way.
Be like bamboo
that achieves growth
through flexibility
and upward action.

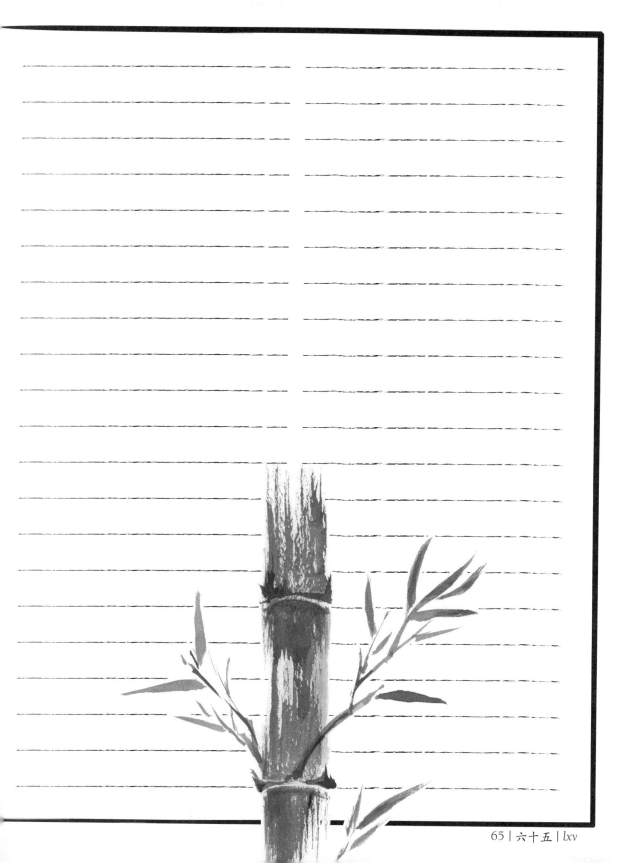

Embrace your imaginative power and do not resist letting in that which wants to be let in.

TODAY IS THE BRIDGE TO TOMORROW.

BE A DELIVERER OF D-I-F-F-E-R-E-N-T.

NOW is the time for action—
NOW is the place for action—
NOW is the need for action.
Stop procrastinating.
Immediately! Your future is
created by how you live
NOW! The actions you take
today will determine your
tomorrows. In order for
success to occur, you must
create a sense of urgency to
do—to act on the great idea
for your life. To delay in taking
direct, assertive action is to
relinquish your well-deserved
right to achieve your deepest
desires.

# NOW is the time for action!

The past is only made of the past. The future is only made of the present. No matter what time of day you check your watch, the only time is now. Time behind is gone, the time ahead is unfixed. Now is the only place in time you have to outwit uncertainty. Living in the now is true living. Learn to regard now as the great gift of opportunity—this is why it is called the present.

# The past is only made of the past.

Be a thinker-upper/writer-downer. Make visible the providential burst that comes to you from out of whatever glorious blue and seize its excitement.

Seeing your idea
on paper will
permit you to
travel beyond
what is into an
exhilarating
world of what
can be.

Do not wait for things to happen to you. Go out and happen to things. Wishing, hoping, waiting for God to smile down will not create an environment where you will flourish. Regardless of your current situation, you must do something toward empowering your idea every day. You simply must accomplish an action.

BE A FANTASY FANATIC.

DREAM BIG. SIZE MATTERS.

Transformation requires ongoing, channeled action. In order for your dream to manifest in the realm of reality, you must act a lot more than a little.

86

八十六

lxxxvi

Too much of life is spent looking for the right answers, when the secret to life lies in being able to ask the right questions. It is the questions we ask or fail to ask that shape our path. Open yourself to awareness. Have the earnestness and the courage to look at your idea honestly, create a list of questions regarding its viability. Do not struggle to figure things out, formulate the questions you are looking to answer and spend the time needed to seek their solution. When we plant a garden of flowers we know not to pull them from the ground in order that they grow faster and taller—we tend to them, nurturing them, seeing that they receive what they require, allowing them to take on a life of their own, blooming fully and naturally.

*We plant a garden of flowers.*

A good idea is
like the river.
With its twists
and turns and its
changes of
direction along
the way, the river
eventually finds
its way to the
sea. A good idea,
like the river,
also finds its
way.

90
—
九十
—
xc

*A good idea is like the river.*

# chop wood

To make the tea, first you must chop the wood and carry the water. Then you must build the fire. Then you must place the leaves into the pot. Then you must wait for the tea to steep. Only when the work is done can the tea be sipped. To truly taste an idea, first you must chop the wood.

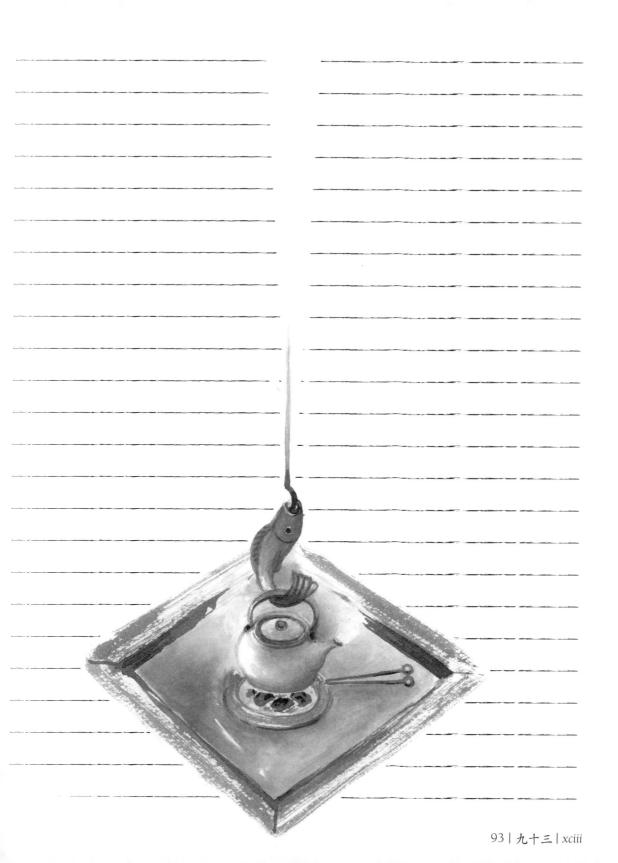

Only into an
empty cup
can the tea
of idea be
poured.
Be open
and empty,
allowing all
possibilities.

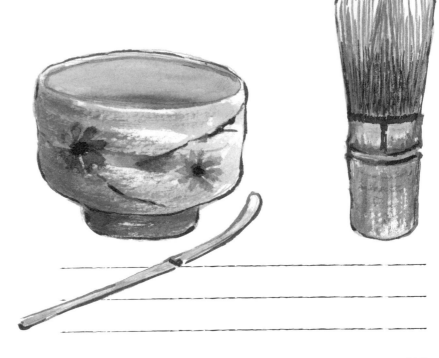

# WHAT IF?

_____
_____
_____
_____
_____
_____
_____

# WHY NOT?

_____
_____
_____
_____
_____
_____
_____

DREAM WILD. BOUNDLESSNESS MATTERS.

The student asks,
"I wonder where the path of an idea can be."
The master points into the air with his staff.
"Here it is."

DREAM **WOW**. WACKINESS MATTERS MOST.

Be flexible with your thinking and your actions. Goals and plans are created. An idea happens. It knows what it needs to realize itself. This means it will call upon you to change. Change is not just the beginning of an idea, but it is the purpose of all ideas.

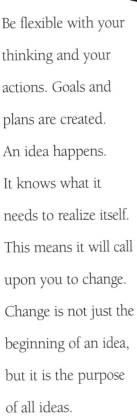

100

百

c

There is no path to an idea; the idea is the path. It is your will and your willingness to make an encounter with the path of awakening and enlightenment that is the true Zentrepreneur's journey. For the person who travels the path with no end, there is always a favorable wind.

An idea is a drama of the visible and the invisible. You mustn't reject anything. Develop confidence in your imagination. No matter how out-of-the-box or foolish your idea may at first appear, write it down. Each idea has within it some useful part that may take you to a higher realm of thought. The knotted and crooked tree is useless to the carpenter but provides inspirational sweeping strokes of beauty for the painter's brush. Ideas visit without call, but only with those who think it important enough to claim them and make work of their inspiration.

# Coming, going, an idea leaves not a trace. Unless it has a guide.

# Sometimes an idea seems impossible.

Sometimes an idea seems impossible. No matter. It is in its very impossibility that we can discover its connection with possibility. Make a list of obstacles that you feel are preventing you from furthering your idea and making it happen. Then create a to-do list of actions that if acted upon would support the potential of your idea. Study the list and you will grasp that this is not a list about what to do but a list of things that need to be done. It is with this realization that wonders soon fall into place.

# MAKE A WORKLIST

| Obstacles | ACTIONS |
|---|---|
|  |  |

110

百十

cx

DELIGHT IN THE OPENNESS OF POSSIBILITIES.

DREAM...THINK...ACT! EVERYTHING ELSE IS MYTHOLOGY.

THINKING OF A NEW IDEA IS MORE INTERESTING THAN LIVING WITH AN OLD ONE.

118

百十八

cxviii

The ancestor. . .

# ACTIONS TO TAKE

to every success is an idea.

THE SECRET TO SUCCEEDING WITH AN IDEA IS IN GETTING THINGS DONE

AN EXIT FROM AN OLD IDEA IS ENTRY TO A NEW ONE

Accomplish  Acquire  Act  Advar

Be  Believe  Build  Choose

Conceive  Consider  Construct

Defend  Declare  Deliver  De

Discover  Discuss  Do  Dream

Enliven  Enthuse  Envision

Find  Facilitate  Further  Ge

Improve  Improvise  Inspire  In

Launch  Make  Motivate  Mov

Persuade  Practice  Prepare

Provide  Pursue  Realize  Refi

Remember  Revise  Study

Think  Train  Understand  Utiliz

Affirm    Ascend    Assert    Aspire

mpion    Claim    Complete    Commit

ntinue    Craft    Create    Decide

    Demonstrate    Desire    Devise

ate    Embrace    Engage    Enhance

ate    Excite    Explore    Express

e    Guide    Illuminate    Imagine

t    Involve    Lead    Learn    Live

Overcome    Perform    Persevere

il    Produce    Progress    Promote

Reflect    Relate    Release

ed    Summon    Sustain    Teach

Verbalize    Visualize    Wonder...

The ancient chartmakers labeled
unexplored waters with the phrase:
"Here be the Dragons." The odyssey of
an idea will take you to places and
times where you will be forced to
confront the dragons of the unknown.
Your mind will see to that. Focus your
energy and trust your instinct. Use
your mind, do not let your mind use
you. Nothing external, no adversity,
difficulty, or doubt can have any power
over you unless you allow it to.

# Zentrepreneur Guides®

## "They're not just books—they're a lifestyle."

**Discover the Journey**. As the proud publisher of this book, we hope that you have been inspired to discover the Zentrepreneur in you. The fact that you purchased the book proves that you are open to your limitless potential. We invite you to read all the Zentrepreneur Guides®, as well as to share them with others.

### Success at Life
#### How to Catch and Live Your Dream

First in the series, guiding you on the importance of finding a mentor, setting goals, resisting negative feedback, avoiding dreamkillers, overcoming obstacles, and pursuing a life of passion.

1-55704-538-0 • $12.95 • Paperback | 1-55704-476-7 • $19.95 • Hardcover

### Dragon Spirit
#### How to Self-Market Your Dream

Second in the series, about the realities of the marketplace, with directions on how to discover the different, create a vision statement, learn the importance of design, build a buzz, and embrace Wow.

1-55704-620-4 • $12.95 • Paperback | 1-55704-563-1 • $19.95 • Hardcover

### Tiger Heart, Tiger Mind
#### How to Empower Your Dream

Third in the series, about learning how to cultivate attitude, take action, form a passion posse, reject fear, determine your direction, undertake the vow of Wow, and establish commitment.

1-55704-621-2 • $19.95 • Hardcover | 1-55704-641-7 • $12.95 • Paperback

### WOWISMS
#### Words of Wisdom for Dreamers and Doers

A perfect-sized giftbook, with more than 130 of the authors inspirational/motivational quotes with 30 beautiful drawings, perfect for graduates, entrepreneurs, and dreamers, young and old.

1-55704-590-9 • $14.00 • Hardcover Gift Book

### The Zentrepreneur's Idea Log & Workbook

An essential belief of the authors is to write things down. "Keep a notebook handy at all times to provide a space for ideas to land." This proactive journal/workbook, illustrated throughout with exquisite zen brush-stroke drawings, was created just for this purpose and is a necessity for budding and experienced Zentrepreneurs.

1-55704-61-7 • $12.95 • Paperback

- **The authors of the Zentrepreneur Guides® Series:** Ron Rubin and Stuart Avery Gold, with anecdotes, humor, and straightforward advice, share their personal experiences and their philosophy of discovery that has made their company, The Republic of Tea, a 21st-century success story (**www.republicoftea.com**).

- **Tell us your story:** We invite you share with us your thoughts and experiences about becoming a Zentrepreneur. The best stories of contributors may be considered for use in future Zentrepreneur Guides®. Ron and Stuart can be reached at **www.zentrepreneurs.com**.

- **Keep up-to-date:** For information and special offers, join our mailing list (we don't sell or pass on mailing list information). Send correspondence to Zentrepreneur Guides®, Newmarket Press, 18 East 48th Street, New York, NY 10017, or sign up at our website **www.newmarketpress.com**.